FIVE FOLD CYCLE

METHOD OF HEALING PERSONAL HURT

KENNETH L. FABBI

Publisher:
Kenneth L. Fabbi
Lethbridge, Alberta, Canada
Email: FiveFoldCycle@gmail.com

Copyright © 2016 by Kenneth L. Fabbi
First Printing — 1990
Second Printing — 2016
Third Printing — 2019 – Revised

All rights reserved.

Unless otherwise indicated, all biblical quotations are taken from the New Revised Standard Version Bible, copyright © 1989 the Division of Christian Education of the National Council of the Churches of Christ in the United States of America. Used by permission. All rights reserved.

Any Internet Address (websites, email, etc.) printed in this book are offered as a resource. They are not intended in any way to be or imply an endorsement by Kenneth L. Fabbi Publishing.

No part of this publication may be reproduced in any form, or by any means, electronic or mechanical, including photocopying, recording, or any information browsing, storage, or retrieval system, without permission in writing from the Author. Kenneth would welcome your communication at FiveFoldCycle@gmail.com.

ISBN:
Hard Cover: 978-0-9952039-0-7
Paperback: 978-0-9952039-1-4
eBook: 978-0-9952039-2-1
Subjects: *Healing Prayer - - Christianity - -*

Problem Solving - - Growth

I. Title   II. Fabbi, Kenneth L.

Table of Contents

Preface	vii
Introduction	xi
The Five Fold Cycle - Diagram	xiii
I. An Understanding of the Background	**1**
1. We are all Broken People	1
2. What do we do to Break out of This Cycle?	2
3. Why do we not Have Perfect Order?	3
4. We Have Free Will and Choice	4
5. The Separation of Body, Mind, Soul, and Spirit	5
We have four basic components:	5
The Web Theory	8
Four Basic Components Explained	10
6. Choices	10
7. So Let's Review	11
Spiritual Law – Negatives are not Under Jesus' Rule	13
Spiritual Law – God Uses all Things	15
II. Process	**17**
Step One: Becoming God Focused	17
Step Two: Identify a Problem or Issue	19
(a) Identify	19
Nibble Theory	20
(b) Sources	20
Plaster Theory	21
(c) Gifts of the Holy Spirit	23

Cube Theory	24
(d) Problems Are Inter-Connected	25
Water Glass and Cube Theory	25
Step Three: Cleaning	26
(a) It's Simple (as all things of God)	26
Spiritual Law: Don't Hold Onto Hurts	27
(b) Don't Dwell	28
(c) Spirits and Bondage	29
(d) Thoughts Cause Feelings	29
Theory Of Nibbling The Cube	30
Spiritual Law: Problems will not be beyond your Strength	31
Step Four: Filling	34
(a) It's Time To Fill	34
(b) Don't Forget The Others	35
(c) Asking	35
(d) Warning	36
(e) You And I Leak	37
Human Sieve	39
Step Five: Thank the Lord	40
III. Instructions	**43**
1. When do you use This Method?	43
2. Let's Look at Depression	45
(a) Anger (Unforgiveness)	46
(b) Guilt	46
(c) Depression	47
3. Mary's Story	47
4. Kora Lynne's Story	49
5. What About Sexual Issues?	53
a) The Homosexual	53
b) The Abused Child	55

6. Dealing with Feelings, Emotions, or Pressures	57
7. My Prayer	61
NOTES:	63

Appendix 'A'
The Five Fold Cycle: Method Of Healing Personal Hurt 67

Appendix 'B'
The Holy Spirit And The Gifts Of The Holy Spirit 71

Appendix 'C'
Every Negative Becomes A Positive In The Cross 75

Appendix 'D'
Supplemental Readings 79

1. Inner Healing References:	79
2. Gifts of the Holy Spirit References:	80
3. Deliverance References:	81
4. Research Review of Interaction of Religion and Health:	81

Appendix 'E'
Scripture as Medicine
The Rx from the Doctor Jesus 83

Preface

When I was beginning my work as a Christian counsellor, I wondered how I would teach people about the wonders of our Lord's healing. I had read many books by people involved in the Christian Healing field, but none seemed to tell people how to do it. They all said things like: "come to the Lord in prayer", "let the Lord take your suffering", "offer it up to the Lord", "give it to the Lord", but no one told you how do to that. I was amazed at all the good ideas and prayerful, holy people; everyone seemed to know that the Lord would fix things, but how?

As I prayed and counselled people, I found that the Lord was showing me simple things regarding prayer, such as images, theories, truths, and methods. All of the knowledge came together as wisdom. In prayer I offered the ideas to very hurting people and the Lord healed them. The miraculous incidents overshadowed the everyday events. Each day it continued to amaze me; some of the miracles were just teasers to encourage us on.

I remember one day when Carol had come by for some prayer; she was worried and depressed that day. When she left, I went back to writing at my desk. I then heard this grinding coming from some car outside. Over and over I heard someone trying to start their car, and the starter ground and ground. Finally it had bothered me enough that I poked my head out, only to find Carol still parked in front of the building. I went over and looked through the open passenger window. "Not starting?" I asked. "Let's say a prayer". Carol was always open to prayer. We said a quick prayer, then she tried the starter again and it started with no trouble. I smiled with amazement. The Lord had encouraged us – it was just a little teaser from the Lord to reassure us that He was around and active.

I became more and more convinced of the power of healing prayer as time went on; the Lord was healing my personal hurts and He was using me to teach others to receive Healing. I started to collect my ideas and put them into a methodology; it was so simple that people didn't believe it would work. I found myself saying hundreds of times, "Just try it! Experiment!" Generally I could get the clients to try it as an experiment. We would do it in my office with the problems they presented to me, and I would challenge them to try it at home. When they came back the next time I would ask how they did, and the majority of the time they said that they had found more peace.

Writing the Method so that people could take it home and put it into their theoretical perspective, came next. It helped me get organized and see the interactiveness of the steps. I thank people like my brother Ron, Maria Lemire, Ron Favreau, and the many clients and friends who taught me and challenged me along the way.

I also thank the Lord, because I know it wasn't me who put this all together. The Lord caused me to teach; He shared His Holy Spirit and the Gifts, and He helped me become systematic. When He set me out to minister to others, I was anything but organized. I was inconsistent, lived a sinful life, and was going nowhere with lots of speed. Today I feel at peace and directed. This comes from the Lord.

I offer the following material to you. I wish and pray that you might find it useful. I ask you to try it out. I ask you to share it with anyone under the Lord's direction. Remember, I am not the Healer, and you are not the Healer. Jesus is the Healer.

You will find that this method is simple, as are all things of the Lord – it will fit into your spiritual life. The Lord will guide you in making it fruitful as long as you listen to Him. Be open to how the Lord wants to deal with you. He deals with each one of us in a personal and private way.

Have fun and enjoy your reading.
– Ken.

Acknowledgements:

The gender, names, locations, professions, ages, and appearances of the persons whose stories are told in this book have been changed to protect their identities, unless they have granted permission to the author or publisher to do otherwise.

A special thanks to Kay Peterson for the original pictures back in 1990 and up-dating some for this edition. And also thanks to Gerben Terpstra for his fine drafting of the Five Fold Cycle Image. I appreciate you folks.

To my Editor, Laura Petker, I want to acknowledge that without your help this material would be very hard to read. Thank you for your professional help!

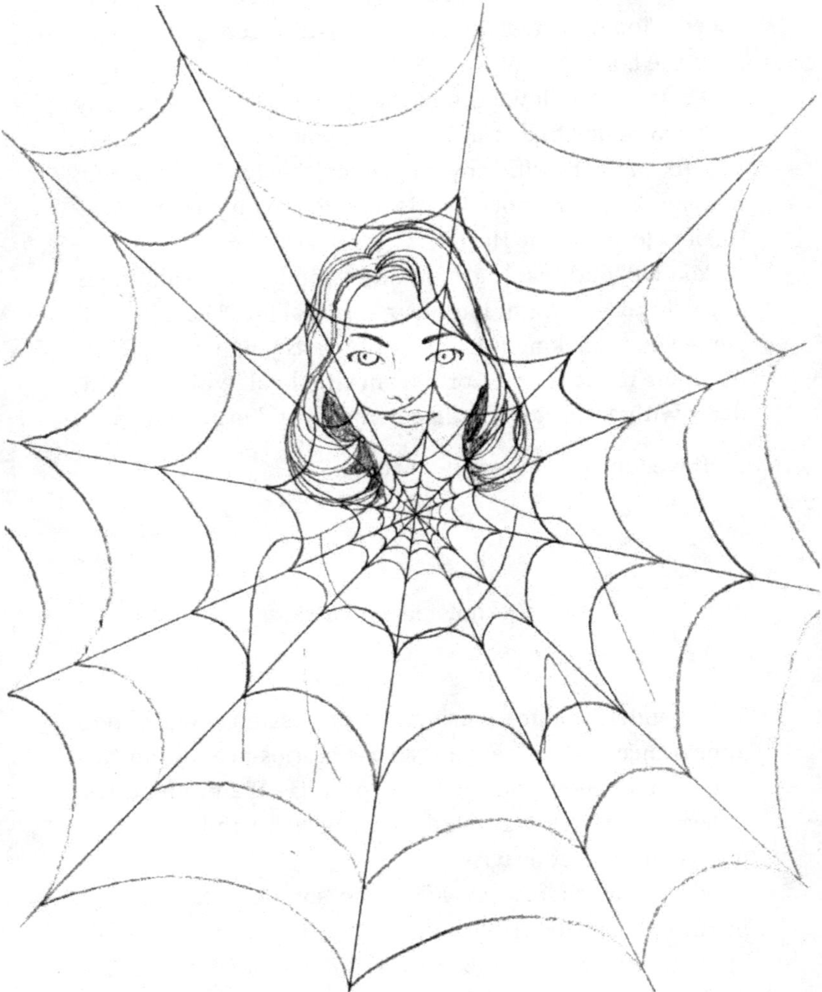

Introduction

In this book I outline a Method of Healing Personal Hurt[1] entitled the "Five Fold Cycle". It is a systems approach to problem solving and is meant to be used to aid in the healing of memories, healing of emotions, healing of self-image, healing of relationships, and other inner healing prayers. It is a method of fine-tuning healing prayer to better utilize the Lord's 'pruning/cleansing'.

Scripture describes the Lord's pruning and cleansing in this manner:

> "I am the true vine, and my Father is the vinegrower. He removes every branch in me that bears no fruit. Every branch that bears fruit he prunes to make it bear more fruit." (John 15:1-2)

It is a simple message from the Lord. He says we are to be *'in Him'* and then he will *'prune'* (cleanse) us.

An old song comes to mind which most adequately describes the process we must use to receive the Lord's cleansing:

> What a friend we have in Jesus
> all our sins and griefs to bear
> What a privilege to carry
> Everything to God in Prayer

> Oh what peace we often forfeit
> Oh what needless pains we bear
> All because we do not carry
> Everything to God in prayer

The process is simple: we must bring each individual issue or problem to the Lord and ask for his help in cleansing it. As we do this we join to Him like a branch to a tree and He joins us, giving us nourishment and peace.

> "Abide in me as I abide in you. Just as the branch cannot bear fruit by itself unless it abides in the vine, neither can you unless you abide in me." (John 15:4)

We also come to realize that we cannot bear fruit, or as the Alcoholics Anonymous movement says: we are powerless unless we abide in Him.

> "I am the vine, you are the branches. Those who abide in me and I in them bear much fruit, because apart from me you can do nothing." (John 15:5)

Let us look at the simplicity of the process God has described for us. I would describe it in this manner:

We come to God in prayer. We focus on an issue or problem, asking for the Lord's help through His Holy Spirit. The Holy Spirit guides us as we take it to the Lord in prayer, asking for cleansing/pruning. After the cleansing we ask the Lord to fill us with His blessings. And finally, we move the focus off of ourselves and refocus on the Lord in thanksgiving and praise.

The Five Fold Cycle - Diagram

METHOD OF HEALING PERSONAL HURT

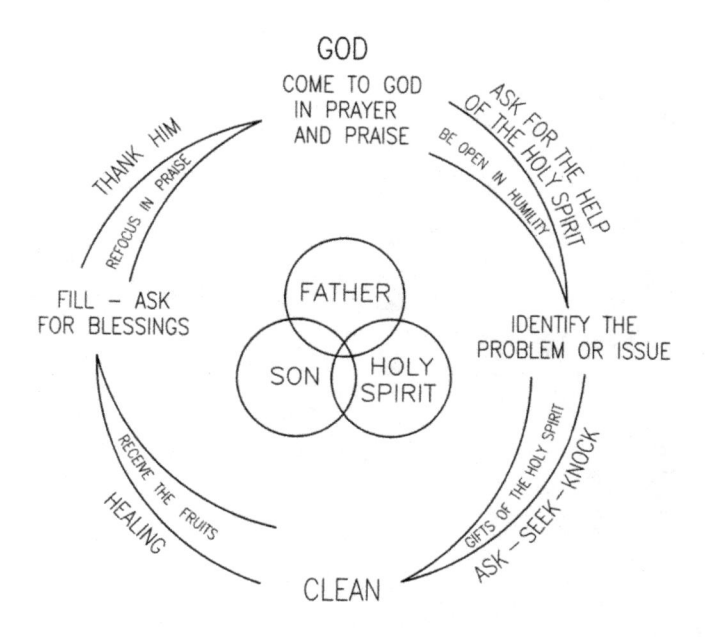

```
                        GOD
                   COME TO GOD
                    IN PRAYER
                    AND PRAISE

        THANK HIM                ASK FOR THE HELP
     REFOCUS IN PRAISE           OF THE HOLY SPIRIT
                                 BE OPEN IN HUMILITY

   FILL – ASK                         IDENTIFY THE
   FOR BLESSINGS      FATHER          PROBLEM OR ISSUE
                   SON   HOLY
                         SPIRIT

     RECEIVE THE FRUITS          GIFTS OF THE HOLY SPIRIT
          HEALING                    ASK – SEEK – KNOCK

                       CLEAN
```

Why do we need inner healing? Why do we need this process? To understand these questions, we must look at the

xiii

scriptural background which leads to the need for this process. Then we will look at the process itself and how the Five Fold Cycle – a problem solving method – is used.

I. An Understanding of the Background

1. We are all Broken People

It doesn't matter who you are, what family you grew up in, nor your financial circumstances – you have been hurt. We are all broken people!

Look back at your parents for a minute. It is often easier to see their brokenness before we can see our own. Each one of your parents had their problems, their hurts, their wounds. Take your mother for instance. What were her wounds? Did she have mother problems? Was there an absence of a mother, or was she overbearing?

Did you pick up her fears, her anger, her bitterness, or maybe her guilt and lack of self-confidence? Take a moment to pause – close your eyes and reflect on the brokenness you received from your mother.

Look at your father. What were his wounds? How did it affect you? Did you learn pride and confidence, or was it fear and mistrust? Was he sensitive and loving, or a tyrant? Or maybe just ineffective? Take a moment to close your eyes, and reflect on your father and the brokenness you received from him.

We are a product of our broken parents they experienced hurt throughout their life, and some of that hurt passed on to us.

Now don't get me wrong, our parents had good points, too. They loved, cared, and nurtured. They did the best with the things they had to offer. But each one of us was wounded. Each one of us is a broken person.

2. What do we do to Break out of This Cycle?

The question comes to mind then: what do we do to break out of this cycle? This is the central question to this book. Through Christ we have been offered a solution to our brokenness:

> "This was to fulfill what had been spoken through the prophet Isaiah, "He took our infirmities and bore our diseases."
> (Mt. 8:17, Is. 53:4-5)

Even back in Isaiah of the Old Testament, it was predicted that Jesus would come and take away our sins and hurts. God is faithful to his promises!

> "Surely he has borne our infirmities and carried our diseases; yet we accounted him stricken, struck down by God, and afflicted. But he was wounded for our transgressions, crushed for our iniquities

upon him was the punishment that made us whole, and by his bruises we are healed."
(Isaiah 53:4-5)

3. Why do we not Have Perfect Order?

Biblical history speaks to us of Adam and Eve as being struck in the likeness of God. If we were then cast in the image of God (Gen. 1:26), then should we not have perfect order? Well yes, but in Genesis Chapter 3 it talks about the fall of Adam and Eve and how this fall has affected all of creation. Basically, we are suffering the effect of their sin. Catholics call this "Original Sin". Paul writes that just like the act 'in Adam' that pulled us down, 'in Jesus' was the act that brought us to life.

> "For since death came through a human being, the resurrection of the dead has also come through a human being; for as all die in Adam, so all will be made alive in Christ." (1 Cor. 15:21-22)

We do not have perfect order because at first we are 'in Adam'. In his fall our spiritual nature became separated from God. The consequence of his action was spiritual death, as well as physical death. 'In Christ' we are reunited; we receive healing and life.

4. We Have Free Will and Choice

God gave us free will. With this free will we are left to choose to follow God and His commandments, or follow our own worldly pursuits.

DIAGRAM - CHOICE LINE

GOD'S LIGHT

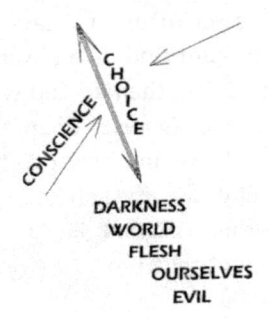

CONSCIENCE   CHOICE

DARKNESS
WORLD
FLESH
OURSELVES
EVIL

The choice is left to us, and whatever we choose is what we get. If we choose God, and along with Him Jesus and the Holy Spirit, then we open ourselves to healing and wholeness.

> "It was he who created humankind in the beginning, and he left them in the power of their own free choice. If you choose, you can keep the commandments, and to act faithfully is a matter of your own choice. He has placed before you fire and water; stretch out your hand for whichever you choose. Before each person are life and death, and whichever one chooses will be given."
> (Sirach 15:14-17)

If we choose the world – the flesh, or Mammon – then we will devoid ourselves of wholeness and healing.

The choice is yours; you can't serve two masters (Mt. 6:24). What will you choose? Stop and think about it.

Now, I don't know why the Lord God gave us free choice. If you were God, would you have given humans free choice? But He did, and we have it. And we must put it to good use.

5. The Separation of Body, Mind, Soul, and Spirit

We have four basic components:

i) Body
ii) Mind
iii) Soul [2]
iv) Spirit

If we think of ourselves as these components, then we can more easily understand how choice affects us. As well, we can see how wholeness is accomplished and healing occurs. Watch how your choices affect the different components.

When we make a decision for Christ and the Trinity, our spirit is immediately healed and is united with the Lord. It is the first conversion experience.

OUR SPIRIT ≈ THE HOLY SPIRIT

This is the conversion experience, or 'born again' experience that Christians talk about. Something happens and we feel good. Of course we feel good – how else could we feel in the presence of the Lord?

You see, with the fall of Adam and Eve, we were separated from the Lord (Gen 3:23+). With our free will we can allow our spirit to be reunited with the Lord.

When we make a decision for Christ, our spirit is joined with the Lord, but what has happened to our body? Nothing! Our body is still the same size and same height as it was before. If we had ulcers, we still have ulcers. If we were fat, we still are fat. The conversion did not change our body. We are told to make it a temple fitting the indwelling of the Holy Spirit (1 Corinthians 6: 19-20). This means we are to start taking care of it - eating right, sleeping right, exercising and caring for it. As we do this, our body comes into oneness with our soul.

What about our mind? There is no change that we notice, or is there? We still have the same thoughts we had before, and the same feelings emoted by those thoughts. If we were hurt by someone – for example, if we were sexually abused – we still remember it. We still feel angry, fearful, guilty, mistrusting, hateful towards men or women, have sexual problems, etc. So is our mind the same? We still think about things that are not of God; we still feel anxious, worried, and impatient. So clearly the Fruit of the Spirit [3] is not present, and therefore our mind hasn't changed. Or has it?

Yes, there *has* been a change. There are new thoughts. When we made the decision for the Lord, the Holy Spirit gave us gifts. Only at this point, they are not encompassing our life. Many of the gifts have not been activated.

Father John H. Hampsch, C.M.F.,[4] explains the position

in which we find ourselves as 'not fully operative'. The gifts and fruit of the Holy Spirit are available to us, but we have not put them into use. Fr. Hampsch explained it as like receiving a gift from a friend and placing it upon a shelf. We have the gift, but it is still fully packaged and wrapped.

If you do not understand what is meant by gifts and fruit of the Holy Spirit, I recommend you review Appendix 'B'. Further depth of understanding maybe obtained by reading T. W. Roycroft's book *You Can Minister Spiritual Gifts* that was republished by this author. If you are Catholic you might read Fr. Robert DeGrandis' books: *Introduction to the Catholic Charismatic Renewal*, *Growth in the Spirit*, and *Layperson's Manual for the Healing Ministry*.[5] If you are Protestant or Anglican/Episcopal, I recommend you read Dennis and Rita Bennett's books: *Nine o'clock In The Morning*, *The Holy Spirit and You*, and *Trinity of Man*.[6]

Our job then is to learn to use the gifts of the Holy Spirit and to begin to live in the fruit of the Holy Spirit.

What about the Soul? [7] Has it changed? No. We still are burdened by the residue of sin that has not been confessed. Things that we have done wrong outside of God's love still plague us, and affect both our mind (guilt) and our body.

One must realize here that all four areas are inter-related, and therefore affect each other.

The Web Theory

It is like a spider web. Every strand is inter-connected to every other strand. Our life is like a web of experiences, memories, emotions, and reactions.

It is easy to see it when we think of how our mind and body are connected, for instance, when we worry we can end up with ulcers. It is a little more difficult to see the other side. An example might be that when we have an injury or the flu, it affects our ability to concentrate and think straight.

In similar ways the soul affects the body and mind, and is affected by the body and the mind in return.

I would guess by this point you are getting the drift - choices affect us in our relationship with the Lord. If we are not in the light of the Lord, then we open ourselves to problems. We have made the wrong choices.

> *But the path of the righteous is like the light of dawn, which shines brighter and brighter until full day. The way of the wicked is like deep darkness; they do not know what they stumble over. (Prov. 4:18-19)*

When we choose the Lord, our spirit is immediately united with Him. This starts the process of the conversion of the other areas of mind, body, and soul.

Scripture tells us to renew our minds; we are told to put on new minds and get rid of the old. This means that we are to allow the Lord's light into old memories, old emotions, old thoughts, and the old automatic behaviors we are used to. As we do this, the Lord starts to renew those thoughts, memories, and emotions. The old automatic behaviors (reactions, retorts, and reflexes) are transformed and changed in the Lord's light. So gradually, our mind is renewed and brought into unity.

We are also told to make our body a temple of the Holy Spirit. This means we are to re-evaluate how we are taking care of our bodies; we must start making them temples worthy of the Holy Spirit. This means eating right, sleeping right, exercising, and caring for our bodies; it may also mean medical care. We start to renew our bodies and bring them into unity.

The soul, as the collector of sin, needs to be cleansed. We need to bring each and every sin to the Lord's light and ask forgiveness. As we cleanse the sin, the soul becomes united with the other parts.

Gradually, all the parts of body, mind, soul, and spirit, come in to unity and oneness with the Lord through the Holy Spirit.

Until we bring the parts into unity with the Spirit there is dissonance, and the dissonance causes confusion and unsettled feelings. Often this dissonance leads people to think that they were not saved by their decision for the Lord. The problem is that they did not follow through on their choice; they did not cleanse the body, mind, and soul.

We must take each area to the Lord, little by little, and bring it under His Light and Lordship (His rule). Each is a mini-conversion experience – dying to self, renewing the old.

Four Basic Components Explained

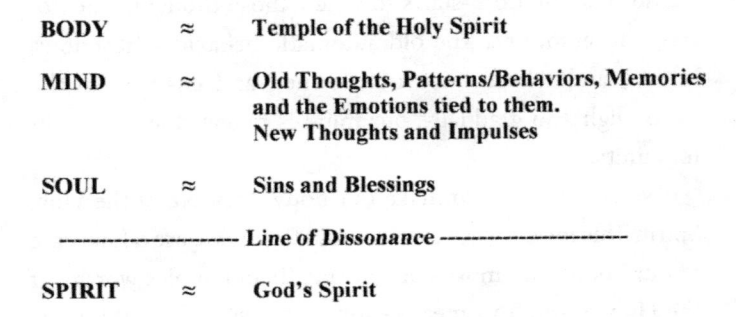

BODY	≈	Temple of the Holy Spirit
MIND	≈	Old Thoughts, Patterns/Behaviors, Memories and the Emotions tied to them. New Thoughts and Impulses
SOUL	≈	Sins and Blessings
---------------------- Line of Dissonance ----------------------
SPIRIT	≈	God's Spirit

6. Choices

The very first choice which predisposes all others is a choice for Christ Jesus. Underlying that is our understanding that Jesus is God and the second Person of the Blessed Trinity (God the Father, Son, and Holy Spirit).

The next stage of choice is turning to God in each event of our life: thought, word, and action. All are mini-conversion experiences. In this way we can begin to experience the new man, and the radical change that Christ promised.

A friend and I were climbing a mountain one day, and as we approached the summit of a ridge he became gripped by fear, which had been building up as we climbed higher and higher. The fear was now overpowering and he was anxious and sweating, holding onto the bushes and trees for all his worth. I had known about his fear of heights, but he had never let me pray and I always assumed he would do the healing prayer himself. The fear, however, had taken him over and he was not enjoying the mountain nor the view from the ridge that looked down to a pristine lake. I offered to pray.

Now you will note that I use the word "simple" when referring to the things of God – because the things of God *are* simple. Read, for example, this scripture: 'perfect love casts out fear' – or we might say 'Love drives out all fear'. (1 John 4: 18) It is a simple equation – love and fear are opposites. But back to the story.

We stopped, closed our eyes, focused on the fear, and looked for the source. The source turned out to be an incident that occurred when he was a young farm boy; he was jumping off the front of a swather and fell, hitting the dirt. It was a small incident in a child's life, but left him with a fear of heights. This fear developed and grew as he grew up.

He had a choice: to keep the fear, or to let the Lord into it. We prayed, asking the Lord into the memory – bringing it to the light. We asked for his grace and peace to fill the boy and commanded the fear to leave. It took only a moment; the fear left and the mountain experiences from then on became exhilarating. It is funny how simple that was in the Lord Jesus!

7. So Let's Review

We are all broken people because we are the products of broken people – our parents. We all receive the effects of being 'in Adam'. We are told in scripture to come to be 'in Jesus'. We are told to join Him as a branch is joined to a tree, and that the Father will cleanse and prune us. That old song 'What A Friend We Have In Jesus' spoke about Jesus as our friend, bearing our sins and griefs. All we have to do is carry them to Him in prayer. When we don't, we suffer needless pain. It is simple.

We learned that we have free will and that we have choices before us. The choices affect us by bringing us under the Lord's light and healing influence, or by inhibiting our ability to receive His love. The results of our choices, and the resultant thoughts, words, and actions, affect our body, mind, soul, and spirit. They are all interactive like the lines of a spider web. Therefore, choices affect our relationship with the Lord.

In each incident in our life, we must choose to move closer to Christ and away from darkness. We do this by involving Him in each incident, each memory, each feeling, and each thought. As He comes into each of these incidents or events, whether in the present or the past, we are transformed by His light.

A PIE

The image of a homemade pie helps me to understand this concept. Picture a pie with pieces cut by some well-intentioned young child. Notice they are irregular and that there are some good size pieces for us sweet-tooths.

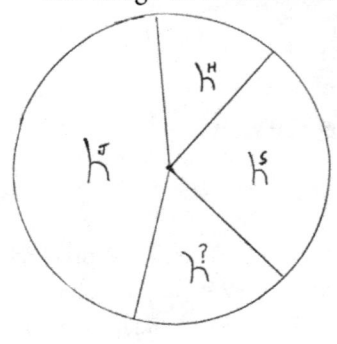

Now let us say this pie represents your relationship

with the Lord. In each section something has to be on the throne. Is it you, God, Money, the World, or what?

Put Jesus – 'J' – on the throne in the largest piece. That is where most Christians would have Him. So in reality, Jesus owns the majority of the pie. But who is on the throne in the other pieces? I put an 'H' on the throne in one piece. That might represent a hurt that you have had in life. Because we were hurt, we did not receive what we needed in that portion of our life. I explain it this way: Jesus wasn't fully able to touch this incident or event, or He wasn't *fully* in that incident or event. If we didn't experience love, joy, peace, and patience - the fruit of the spirit, then Jesus healing touch was inhibited. That is why we feel hurt.

Look at another section of the pie. I put an 'S' on that one. It stands for 'sex'. In my life, and I am sure in the lives of others, Jesus didn't always have control of our sex life. Therefore, he wasn't on the throne. We have to let him on the throne in the present and in the past. As He heals us, He will take over that portion of the pie, and we gradually nibble away at the problem areas.

We want the Lord to take over all our lives and be active in each portion of the pie. Then we will be in unity, and we will find love, joy, peace – The fruit of the Spirit - flowing throughout us, body, mind, soul and spirit. The Lord will make our personalities more integrated and more whole.

There is a spiritual law that applies to our lives:

Spiritual Law – Negatives are not Under Jesus' Rule

If you find that any Portion of your Life does not have the Fruit of the Spirit, then Jesus isn't fully present.

Paul put it quite succinctly in Ephesians, where he told us to take off the old and put on the new:

> "You were taught to put away your former way of life, your old self, corrupt and deluded by its lusts, and to be renewed in the spirit of your minds, and to clothe yourselves with the new self, created according to the likeness of God in true righteousness and holiness." (Eph. 4:22-24.)

Paul tells us to put on a new mind, and he tells us to transform our mind. He is talking about a process of overcoming the old self – the Old Man. As we go through this process, we become renewed, but it is not instantaneous. In the born-again experience we feel a change and often it stays with us for quite a while. But gradually the old feeling, thoughts, and actions come back to haunt us. There is a dissonance between the areas where Christ is on the throne and the other parts of our lives. That is where inner healing comes in to fill the gap. Jesus' love is not caught up in time and space; He can 'renew' our minds, our hurts, and our bodies. All we have to do is allow Him into the negative things in our lives.

There is a second spiritual law that reassures us that even the most hideous sin can be renewed by the Lord's love:

Spiritual Law – God Uses all Things

God uses all things unto good for those who love Him.

The story of Joseph, who was sold into slavery, is a fine example of how God can use anything unto good (Gen. 37+). He repeats this promise at least three times in scripture (Rom. 8:28, Is. 38:17, Gen. 50:20).

We must take heart and trust in the unfailing love of the Lord who will transform us.

In Part II the book will outline the process involved in the Method of Healing Personal Hurt – Five Fold Cycle.

CHRIST BEFORE THY DOOR IS WAITING
—by W. Rainey, circa 1883.

II. Process

We will now look at a step by step method of healing personal hurt, called: The Five Fold Cycle.

Step One: Becoming God Focused

> The Lord lives in the praises of his people.
> (Author Unknown)

I am not sure where that phrase came from, but it is obvious that as we turn our attention to the Lord, He joins with us in a special way.

> "Listen! I am standing at the door, knocking; if you hear my voice and open the door, I will come in to you and eat with you, and you with me." (Rev. 3:20).

Turning to God is using our free will, to open ourselves to the Lord. It reminds me of the painting of Christ standing outside the door and knocking. If we do not open the door, he will not come in.

Often in these paintings there is no doorknob on the side where Jesus Christ is standing. The artist is implying that we must open the door – that our choice opens the door and that Christ waits patiently, arms outstretched and with His love flowing. All we need to do is open the door a little ways, or throw it wide open. It is up to us to choose.

> "So I say to you, Ask, and it will be given you; search, and you will find; knock, and the door will be opened for you." (Luke 11:9)

I refer to this repeatedly, because asking is the 'key' to personal healing in Christ. Each time we ask we are choosing God, and therefore we are receiving more, finding more, and opening more. Each is a mini-conversion experience. The first step we must take is to focus on God. We pray and praise Him in whatever way is natural to us, and the Lord will hear.

> "And this is the boldness we have in him, that if we ask anything according to his will, he hears us. And if we know that he hears us in whatever we ask, we know that we have obtained the requests made of him." (1 John 5:14-15.)

I remember an incident at a weekend youth event. It was late in the evening, and I came to the top landing of a set of stairs to find a teen sitting with his legs dangling through the banister. His head was down and he seemed troubled, separated from the group. I approached him to find out how he was doing and he said he had a headache. Now I know headaches are no problem for the Lord, so I asked him if I could pray for him. The young man had not prayed, but was very open to it. We prayed for just a moment but that was all it took – the headache was gone. I remember his excitement and his witness, as he ran around the place telling everyone what had just happened. All that was needed was one thing – simply turning to God and asking for His help!

Step Two: Identify a Problem or Issue

(a) Identify

At this point we identify a problem we are having in our life, or an issue which is interfering with our peaceful walk with the Lord.

It has become evident to me and my colleagues that you have to pick small things and be as specific as possible.

Now I know the Lord can do anything He wants. If He can create you, me, and the world, He could fix something as complex as a marital problem; but it doesn't seem to work that way. It seems that our job is to divide the big events into smaller events. It is like dissecting a specimen in biology.

DIAGRAM – WEDGE

A picture here would be useful. First, think of a marriage as a dot, where two people come together. Then as their marriage progresses, little problems and issues come up. I call that "garbage". The garbage builds up, separating the two lines (people). It ends up looking like a wedge from the pie, with all sorts of junk in the middle.

Now the garbage can be as little as not resolving the issue around how to clean your tooth brush, or how to squeeze the toothpaste tube. The issue just gets packed away and is not resolved. It is just another speck of garbage.

But sooner or later the garbage can gets full, and then it becomes overwhelming.

In the problem solving process, it is necessary to be specific and begin to nibble away at the issues one at a time. As you do this, the lines (people) come together, as represented in the diagram below, entitled "Nibble Theory".

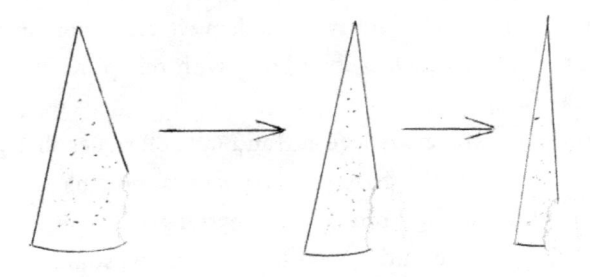

NIBBLE THEORY

(b) Sources

In the process of identification, we want to get to the root of the problem – we are looking for the source. If you can get to the root of the problem, you and the Lord can clean it up.

PLASTER THEORY

A picture might be helpful here. Think of a house where there is a crack in the foundation; it is inevitable that the crack will run up the plaster wall. You can patch the plaster all you want, but it just cracks open shortly after. To fix the problem once and for all, you have to fix the foundation. Then when you fix the plaster, it remains fixed.

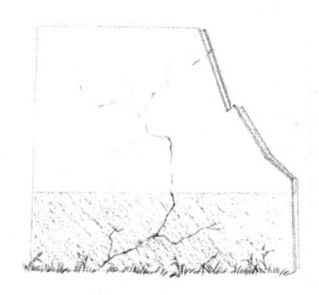

We humans are not much different. We have to get back to the original injury (cracks), if we really want healing.

You will have to use your discretion here because sometimes you have to work back a step at a time, and other times you can start at the root and come forward. Prayer for help from the Holy Spirit would be useful at this point, in order to provide Knowledge and Wisdom.

A prompting that often comes to mind in counselling at this point is *'ask the Lord where you first experienced this feeling, emotion, thought, or issue'*. The source of many issues goes back to earlier life experiences, which are the foundations that we build our life upon. When the foundational experience is negative – the opposite of love, joy, peace, patience, gentleness and self-control – we then have a root that will negatively affect our life.

I remember an experience that I had one day when I was walking downtown for coffee. I heard the sound of the large plastic-insert on the commercial business sign squeaking in the wind. I instantly looked over my shoulder, expecting something to happen. It was an automatic response. But why? Why did I look back?

Later in the day when I had time to reflect, I posed the question to the Lord through His Holy Spirit (Become God Focused and Identify): why did I look back? Immediately a memory came to mind. When I was just a little guy in the Okanagan fruit orchards of British Columbia, my brother, young uncle and I, were building a tree house in one of my grandfather's apple trees.

When he saw what we had done, my grandfather got quite angry and ordered us to take it down. You see, the branches of an apple tree can't handle much weight, especially the weight of a tree house. So my brother, uncle and I headed out to take it down. I stayed below, and they went up the tree and began to remove the boards and nails. When they pulled out the nails, they made a sound just like the plastic in commercial signs when the wind blows.

You can probably guess what happened! It was my job to pick up the boards that they threw down and pile them up neatly. At one point I got under the tree too early; I heard the sound of the nails just before I got hit. I was bent over when the board hit my head, and my head began to bleed. It caused quite an uproar in the family, as I remember.

So there it is. The noise from the sign set off a negative memory with which fear and hurt was involved. It somehow resulted in an automatic behavior, where I would look over my shoulder when I heard this particular squeaking sound; there were no emotions attached, just this odd reflex behavior.

I prayed, asking the Lord into my experience (Becoming God Focused), and asked Him to take the fear and hurt away (Cleaning). I then asked that He fill it with His love and peace (Filling). I have never had a repeat experience with the squeaking sound since that day.

We must remember, however, that everything is inter-connected. Remember the spider web (Web Theory in Section I). One injury attaches to another, and each event in life is connected to the next. Therefore, problems can get quite confusing. It is important to be as specific as possible and only deal with one issue at a time.

The simplest way to deal with inter-connected issues is jot them down and then deal with one at a time.

(c) Gifts of the Holy Spirit

Often we need help in the identification process, as it can be confusing. We sometimes don't remember things and our mind has ways of jumbling everything up. Confusion is a very common problem.

One must remember that every experience we have is kept in the memory. In psychological studies they have touched probes in the brain, and different areas elicited different memories. They can come in colour, with sound, and even smell.

It reminds me of one time when I was walking down the street and I heard a song from my high school days; it reminded me of old memories I had forgotten. I am sure you have had a similar experience where something brought up a memory, names, faces, and experiences you had long forgotten.

CUBE THEORY

The memory is like an ice cube. Only a little of the cube is above the water line. That is the conscious memory. Below the surface is the largest part of the cube and that is our unconscious memory. It is a good image.

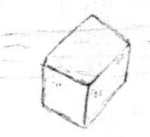

With this image and theory in mind it becomes obviously that we need some help from the Lord. The source of the Lords help is His Holy Spirit, who is our Comforter, Teacher and Advocate.

If you look in 1 Corinthians 12 - 14 it talks about the Gifts of the Holy Spirit. They are there for the asking. The Gifts we need in this case are the gifts of Understanding: both Knowledge and Wisdom. (1 Cor. 12:8).

Now the Lord answers prayers and he does it quite simply. You ask and then listen for a reply. The reply can come in many ways: a single word, a complete thought, a feeling, a picture or vision. The Lord can use anything and anyone. You have to be open to the Lord's Gifts. You have to listen and be attentive.

The Letter of James provides the promise; reassuring us that God will provide the information when we ask.

> "If any of you is lacking in wisdom, ask God, who gives to all generously and ungrudgingly, and it will be given you." (James 1:5)

The corollary is 'if you don't ask you don't receive'. Now that is not perfectly true but the scripture could be written to say: 'If you don't ask you don't receive, if you don't seek you won't find and if you don't knock no one will answer the door'.

It gets to be exciting as we fine tune the Gifts and learn how the Lord speaks to us. He answers prayers!

Some books that you might enjoy in this healing prayer area are listed in the Supplemental Readings - Appendix 'D'.

(d) Problems Are Inter-Connected

There is another image you need to see to understand what happens with human problems. The image is that of a water glass with a lot of ice cubes.

WATER GLASS and CUBE THEORY

In a glass, sometimes the ice cubes bump and stick together. The same thing happens with our problems. For example, jealousy might attach to a fear you have, and as a result you have a more confusing problem.

Our job in this stage is to identify and separate the problems and issues into small manageable portions, and then take them one by one to the Lord.

Step Three: Cleaning

(a) It's Simple (as all things of God)

When we notice that something is wrong, our job is to 'do something' about it – we have to make a choice. The choice predicates an action, and the action is to bring it to the Lord and clean it up with His help.

First, we bring the problem to Him in prayer. If we are at fault, we ask the Lord for forgiveness. If it is someone else's fault, we forgive them and ask the Lord to forgive them.

Forgiveness here might apply to ourselves, to others, or even to God. As this book was not intended to teach forgiveness, I would recommend Fr. Robert DeGrandis' books[8], *Forgiveness and Inner Healing*, *To Forgive is Divine*, or *Brokenness to Life*.

The important point here is that we do whatever is necessary to clean ourselves and everyone else who comes into our minds eye.

Sometimes it helps to picture the situation in your mind and pretend that you are house cleaning. Cleaning might go like this:
- We confess our sins.
- We ask for cleansing.
- We give the problem up to the Lord, for instance, worry and anxiety.

- We ask the Lord to take away any negatives, such as anger, fear, jealousy, hurt, loss of self-esteem, loss of love, revenge, loss of memory, infantile habits, confusion, etc.
- We give up any childhood vow made in such an incident.
- Watch for decisions made which have foundations built on hurts; generally they are always harmful. Clean them up by releasing them to the Lord.

Remember the spiritual law that applies:

Spiritual Law: Don't Hold Onto Hurts

Jesus has Taken all our Hurts and Sickness when He Died on the Cross (Ref: Mt. 8:17, Is. 53:4).

It is often important to follow through by personal contact with the parties involved, but remember to use discretion and discernment.

If you find it difficult to do this step by yourself, find a prayer partner. You might also refer to the '12 Steps' of the Alcoholics Anonymous movement. It is an excellent method of cleansing.

Another important tool in cleansing is "Sacrament Confession", or "Reconciliation". You will note that it is similar to the Alcoholics Anonymous method: "Admitting to God, to ourselves, and to another human being the exact nature of our wrongs" (A.A. Step 5).

(b) Don't Dwell

It is not good to dwell on evil and the horrors of the past. This cleansing can take a moment, or it might take days of quick little prayers.

An example of how simple it can be goes like this: you are driving down the road and someone cuts you off. You immediately get angry and you raise your fist. Clearly your anger is not exhibiting God's love or God's light for that second. So what do you do? As soon as you notice the incongruence, you say:

> 'Lord be with me', (Become God Focused).
> 'I bring this incident to you', (Identification of the Problem).
> 'I am sorry for my anger, forgive me', (Cleansing).
> 'Lord give me your love and your peace', (Filling).

Then you should clean up the others hurt in the situation:

> 'The other driver was hurt by my anger, cleanse him Lord', (Cleansing and Intercessory Prayer).
> 'Bless him Lord', (Filling).

If your child was beside you in this incident of rage, what would have happened to them? Would they have picked up that rage? In that event the child must be cleansed of their hurt, because they would have felt that anger.

Finally, you say 'thank you Lord', (Thank you Prayer).

Now how long did that take? Two seconds. It is quite easy, as are all things of the Lord.

You might want to look at Appendix 'A' - The Five Fold Cycle: Method of Healing Personal Hurt at this time. The Five Fold Cycle is meant as a tool you can pass on to others as part of your healing outreach.

Now you're cleansing could get very long if you are dealing with an abuse situation, but just be patient and do things in God's time and God's peace. There is no rush to solve all of your problems the first time you sit down.

(c) Spirits and Bondage

Sometimes, however, things have gone too far, and with simple prayer you cannot get release. This is where deliverance prayer comes into play. Fr. Michael Scanlan and Randall Cirner have a good book[9] that covers this topic, called *Deliverance From Evil Spirits*. The issue in dealing with spirits and bondage, is to use the power that the Lord Jesus gave you and His apostles through his shedding of blood. You bind spirits and release or sever bondage in the name of Jesus; you then give them to Jesus to dispose of as He wishes. For more information on this topic you might look at Appendix 'D' Supplemental Readings, Section 3. entitled Deliverance References.

(d) Thoughts Cause Feelings

This concept is important. Thoughts cause feelings; if you don't have thoughts, you don't get feelings. Of course, once the feelings start rolling you can jump all over the place, because everything is inter-connected. Remember the Spider Web Theory.

When you are identifying a problem or issue, look for a single source: is it a thought or memory? Then jot down the feelings that it emotes.

For Example: Someone Hits You

Negatives:
- I am angry
- I feel sorry for myself
- I am confused
- I want to get back
- I feel doubt
- I fantasize aggression

We clean each emotion or reaction by bringing it to the Lord, then we go on to the next thought. There is a complication here, however – emotions can attach to each other, just like problems can. You will remember the Theory of the Water Glass and Cubes. The solution is the same – divide them up and deal with them individually.

You will remember the Ice Cube Theory. If you think of fear as an ice cube, what happens when you nibble a corner of it? The ice cube rises, and other related experience comes to the surface.

THEORY OF NIBBLING THE CUBE

Don't worry if new things rise to the conscious memory – it is normal. As you nibble away, you will get rid of the whole ice cube.

There is another Spiritual Law and Promise from the Lord:

Spiritual Law: Problems will not be beyond your Strength

You can trust God not to let you be tried beyond your strength, and with any trial, He will give you a way out of it, and the strength to bear it. (1 Cor. 10:13)

The Cleansing Step is then simply a process of asking and seeking the Lord's help. He has assured us that if we ask we will receive, and that we can trust in him to take us through any burden that comes our way. What a wonderful assurance.

Here is an example of how this cleaning process might go. Ron, a friend, dropped into my office one day, very upset. Ron had been studying for an insurance/mutual fund exam and said that "every time he closed the book, he could not remember anything he had studied". He said that he was "so frustrated and ready to quit".

We followed the procedure in the Five Fold Cycle. First we prayed, asking the Lord in and asking for His guidance (God Focused). I asked Ron to focus deeply on what he felt when he thought of his exams, and to ask for the help of the Holy Spirit to know when he had experienced that feeling before (Identify the Problem).

With only a moment of reflection, Ron remembered a time when he was a teen coming home with his report card. He found his father in the backyard and showed him the card. His father read it and stated, "you'll never make it".

Some Christian counsellors call this a curse. A father's role is to bless, lift up his child out of the mother's arms, encourage the child to stand, to walk, and to be secure and confident. This father had not blessed but put on shackles of discouragement – by saying that "you'll never make it" and that you are unable.

Ron remembers being crushed and lying against the big tree in the middle of the yard. His mind was set, his course was set, he could never succeed. He was useless!

We took these negative and false beliefs to Jesus on the cross (Cleaning). We gave them to Jesus and forgave Ron's father, and asked that he be blessed. We ask the Lord to replace the feeling of inability with Ron's true ability (Filling). We prayed to bless his mind, his memory, and his recall under the stress of exams. We prayed to bless his ability to read, study, and remember. Ron passed the exam!

Through intercessory prayer we use the same process of cleaning to clean and heal the others in our story, in this case Ron's father.

The scripture that can be applied here is from Matthew 5:13-16 which talks about each one of us being 'Salt and Light' in the world:

> "You are the salt of the earth; but if salt has lost its taste, how can its saltiness be restored? It is no longer good for anything, but is thrown out and trampled under foot.
>
> "You are the light of the world. A city built on a hill cannot be hid. No one after lighting a lamp puts it under the bushel basket, but on the lampstand, and it gives light to all in the house. In the same way, let your light shine before others, so that they may see your good works and give glory to your Father in heaven." (Mt. 5:13-16)

The same promises previously mentioned (Luke 11:9 and 1 John 5:14-15), can be brought to bear on the lives of people around us. Like in Ron's story where we prayed for his father, it is our responsibility to be the light and the salt of the world. In this case we used a negative experience as a turning point, to pray as intercessors for Ron's father, asking forgiveness and healing to the father and the father relationship.

As we intercede for others, we spread this light and salt to the world around us. You will be surprised how your seemingly simple little prayers for people around you affect their anger, their fear, their guilt, and the like!

I remember being with a young boy who was having trouble reading the situations around him, and as a result that caused him difficulties in the playground because he hogged the ball and didn't share. We went to a mall and I pointed out obvious problems with people around us, and then we did intercessory prayer for the situation. The idea was to teach him how to read situations and discern others.

That day there was a mother sitting in the cafeteria with two children; she was obviously depressed. We started praying for the mother, asking that the depression be taken off her and blessing the children, who had way too much energy for someone in that condition. In just a couple minutes someone walked up to her and began to talk to her – it was like the light of God arrived. The mother's face lit up and there was a peace around her and the children. Prayer was answered!

In grief or rejoicing, fear or thanksgiving, guilt or uncertainty, we are always welcome to turn to our Father.

Step Four: Filling

(a) It's Time To Fill

In Step 3, we talked about cleaning as if you were cleaning the house. After you are finished cleaning the problem, it is important to fill it up. It is like when you are stopping a little child from touching a hot stove – you redirect or give them something to replace that negative interest, like a sucker or toy.

In filling, we are replacing the negative things with positives, with the Lord's help. In the world of the Holy Spirit, the positives are the fruit found in Galatians:

> "... the fruit of the Spirit is love, joy, peace, patience, kindness, generosity, faithfulness, gentleness, and self-control..." (Galatians 5:22-23).

For example, if we have cleaned away fear, we ask the Lord for his love. If we have cleaned away guilt, we ask the Lord to replace it with good feelings about our-self.

Doubt with assuredness and certainty.

Confusion with understanding and confidence.

Lack of trust with trust.

Anger with forgiveness and love.

Just use your imagination, remembering that the Lord wants the best for us and He wants us to be whole, for he has promised to give us all things:

"If you abide in me, and my words abide in you, ask for whatever you wish, and it will be done for you." (John 15:7)

"O Lord my God, I cried to you for help, and you have healed me." (Psalm 30:2)

(b) Don't Forget The Others

When you were cleaning yourself, you also cleaned the others in the situation. So when you fill, you need to fill the others. This is called "intercessory prayer". You as an intercessor; pray for their blessing, as well as your own. You will find that prayers are answered.

My brother always says that the prayer of family members is powerful. So test this – have a child pray for a father or a husband pray for his wife. It is exciting, and the Lord will bless your prayer.

(c) Asking

Underlying the filling process is the need for you to ask of the Lord. 'Ask and you will receive'. Have you noticed how many times the Lord told you to ask?

Here are a few references: Mt. 7:7
                               Mt. 18:19
                               Mk. 11:24

> Lk. 11:9
> Jn. 14:13
> Jn. 15:7
> Jam. 4:2 - 3
> 1 Jn. 3:22
> 1 Jn. 5:14

After that many hints, you would think we would get the message. It is like He gave us a 13th commandment: 'ask of the Lord your God, Who would love to give to you'.

(d) Warning

If you clean the problem or issue and do nothing to replace them with positives (blessings), there is a high probability that you can slip back into the same old routines.

One must fill the place that has been cleaned with the good things from God, through His Holy Spirit.

In serious situations the filling process is not a one-time event. As we fill one event, our memory brings a related issue to our mind and we continue until we are clear. When we identify serious issues or problems, we must continually fill them through prayer and scripture. I have used a system for many years called "Scripture as Medicine", a teaching from Fr. John Hampsch.[10] Because it is a very effective method, I have attached it as Appendix E. It outlines how to use the promises of scripture.

If we do not fill we will not retain the cleansing nor will we be able to resist the temptation and spiritual attacks which will bombard us in the days to follow.

We must remember we are in a spiritual battle and the only way to win is to keep our armor in good order. (Ep. 6:10 ff.).

(e) You And I Leak

I like to picture myself as a human sieve – basically we all leak. Because we leak, we have to keep topping up the blessed fluid. How do we do that? We cannot get it by our efforts alone, but only by the grace of God. We must continually *ask*, we must take part in the Sacraments and attend church, we must pray and worship, and we must read the Word and apply it in our life. Communion is a "High Octane Filling Station" in the filling process.

As we do these things, the Lord will continue to top up the blessed fluid.

A story might help to explain this idea of the Human Sieve. I remember one day when I was heading downtown to meet some friends for coffee. One of the parents from the youth group had done some t-shirt designs for me and I was carrying the designs to show folks what had been created for the youth. These were hand-made, embroidered designed t-shirts and there were just enough for each of the youth.

I entered the coffee shop and sat down with the ladies; one lady named Aleciah took one of the t-shirts to the next room to show some of her friends. When she came back, she did not have the t-shirt and told me that she had sold it. I was mad. Very mad! I grabbed the pile of samples and stormed out of the place, heading to Mass at a nearby Catholic Church.

I was on my knees praying in the church, waiting for Mass to begin, when a friend, Gerben, came up and said he saw a hole right through the middle of my back. As he touched the spot, I winced in pain – it hurt badly. I knew immediately what it was: I was angry at Aleciah and the sale of the t-shirt, and it was lodged in my back.

Now you will remember that I said we are like human sieves. I had let anger take hold and had lost the blessing; I was leaking and I had a hole in my spiritual armor. You usually think of these holes as more symbolic, but this was a hole that when you touched it, it physically hurt – badly.

To heal and fill it, I asked God for forgiveness, I forgave Aleciah, and then went to communion, offering up the sin (Cleaning). As I received communion, the bread of life (John 6:32-35), I asked God to fill the spot (Filling). By the time I reached my seat, the pain had left. Just to make sure I was total healed, I asked my friend to check to see if the hole was still visible, and he said no. He has a wonderful gift, the gift of knowledge, being able to see the spiritual covering around people – you might call it an aura.

HUMAN SIEVE

Step Five: Thank the Lord

Scripture has told us that when we focus on our problems they begin to cloud us; Scripture has also told us to look away from our problems and focus on the Lord.

> "Do not worry about anything, but in everything by prayer and supplication with thanksgiving let your requests be made known to God. And the peace of God, which surpasses all understanding, will guard your hearts and your minds in Christ Jesus." (Phil. 4:6-7)

As you go through the process, you will feel and notice changes. Don't forget to thank the Lord; you thank Him in your words and your praise.

The Five Fold Cycle has now taken us back to where we started – with God. The Five Fold Cycle is a systems theory[11], completed in and through the Lord. Remember the scripture which describes us as branches grafted to Jesus and the Father as the pruner and cleanser:

> "I am the true vine, and my Father is the vinegrower. He removes every branch in me that bears no fruit. Every branch that bears fruit he prunes to make it bear more fruit." (Jn. 15:1-2)

It is a very simple process and easily fits into the ordinary methods of prayer. The process is very simple: you bring your attention to the Lord, you ask for the help of the Holy Spirit to identify the issue or problem, you clean it with the help of the Lord, you fill it with blessings from the Lord, and finally you thank the Lord.

We will now look at examples of real stories to see how the process can be used in practice.

III. Instructions

1. When do you use This Method?

This method has been found to be useful in many areas of healing: healing of memories, healing of emotions, healing of fears and anxiety, healing the self-image, deliverance prayer, and depression, just to name a few.

Any time you are looking to receive something from the Lord you can use this method.

I like to describe its use this way:

Every time you see a negative, whether in thought, memory, emotion, or happening, your job is to go to the Lord and ask for the opposite blessing. You can imagine it this way:

NEGATIVES TO POSITIVES THROUGH THE CROSS

WHENEVER YOU SEE A NEGATIVE

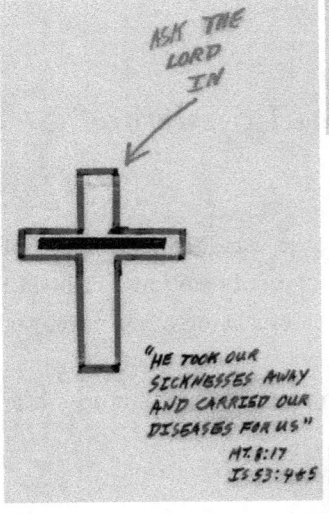

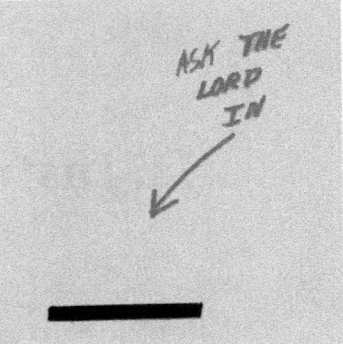

WE BRING IT TO JESUS THROUGH THE CROSS

WE ASK FOR A POSITIVE – THE OPPOSITE GOOD THING

You might look at Appendix 'C' for another explanation of Negatives to Positives through the Cross of Jesus.

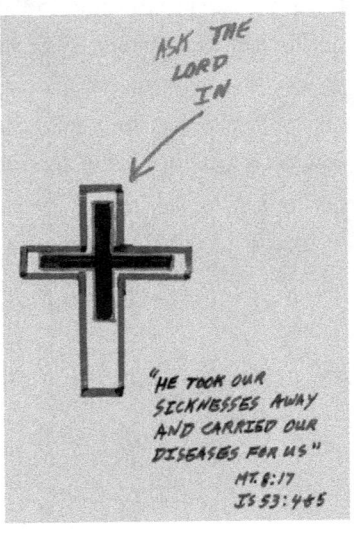

2. Let's Look at Depression

In about 1985 I started training people, who said they were depressed, in The Five Fold Cycle: Method of Healing Personal Hurt.

I learned to see depression in these terms: when we are hurt, there are three negative reactions. I learned that if I taught people to do these simple housecleaning steps, that the depression left.

There are three reactions when we get hurt: anger, guilt, and depression. Anger is outward focused, guilt is inward focused, and depression is the symptom of the two working their havoc on the person and their body.

My brother came up with the following diagram to represent the relationship between them: the two legs of the stool. He calls our anger and guilt a mushroom, or toad stool. The seat/top is contingent on the legs holding it up. The seat/top is depression.

Anger, Guilt and Depression

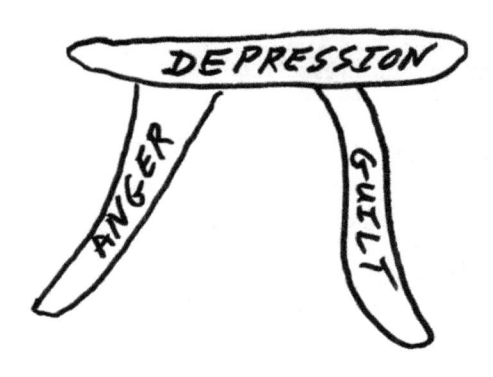

(a) Anger (Unforgiveness)

Anger is a reaction to being hurt. When we are confronted with a negative situation we become angry, bitter, resentful, and the like. We may repress the anger and hurt, but we don't forget it. We have moved out of God's light (by choice) and moved into the darkness. We have not forgiven; our pointer finger is pointing out and we are holding someone guilty, judged. We don't let others off the hook.

Now don't get me wrong – I am not trying to say these people who hurt us weren't wrong; I am not trying to say that the people who hurt us did not sin. The problem is that we are going against God's Law.

(b) Guilt

Guilt is basically taking weight onto our shoulders; it is not forgiving the self. It is worry, self-pity, uncertainty, anxiety, and tension that results from this. It is taking anger and hurt out on ourselves; the pointer finger in this case is pointing at us. We don't let ourselves off the hook.

I like to think of guilt as putting on a cloak. We have the image of Joseph's cloak being the cloak of many colors; the cloak of guilt is more like a heavy weight. It blocks out God's light and it burdens us down. It presses upon us, taxes our strength, and clouds over our mind (Ephesians 4:17+, 1 Corinthians 2: 14 & Isaiah 59:2).

It is evil's oppression.

(c) Depression

Depression in its simplest form is the combination of anger and guilt. The two work together, spinning together to take us down and down into the depths of depression.

You can't do anything about depression because it is a symptom. You can only work on the anger, the guilt, and the unforgiveness. As you clean up each incident of unforgiveness and guilt, the depression is relieved.

The challenge then is to take each little incident or memory and work it through The Five Fold Cycle.[12] Each incident or memory is then used as a mini-conversion experience. We take it to the Lord, we give it to Him, we adhere to His will, and ask for His directions and blessings. Gradually, all our life comes under the Lord's scrutiny and His Healing; the Lord heals the cracks and brokenness by pruning and cleansing each little branch.

When He is finished, even our problems are transformed[13] into blessings.

3. Mary's Story

Mary is a beautiful lady who I met quite a few years ago; at that time she was very depressed and suicidal. She came into my office quite unexpected one day, and cried and cried. Mary had been under a lot of strain, and felt that no one was listening to her. She had been hurt in a car accident, and since then was going from one doctor to another. She took a multitude of pills and tried any treatment she could find, but nothing seemed to be working.

We went into prayer and placed the problem into the Lord's hand, asking for help from the Holy Spirit (Become God Focused and Identify). Mary cried as she retold the many stories of hurt that she held inside. As each was brought out, we prayed for the Lord's healing and released them (Cleaning and Filling). It was wonderful to feel the pressure dropping with each tear that fell to her blouse. As each weight dropped off of her Cloak, she felt better. Twenty minutes went by and she was left smiling.

It was only a short time, however, before Mary was back; she just could not do it herself. There was a heaviness about her and I asked the Lord what it was. The knowledge he gave to me was one word: coffin; I kept this to myself (Use of the Gifts of the Holy Spirit). She began to tell me what she was feeling and how she had started to go on a crash diet to lose weight. She cried and cried, and my heart broke. She asked if I knew why she was doing this, and I said that I did. I felt as though I had to prove the power of the Lord to her, so I did not give her the answer to the question. I wrote the word I had heard from the Lord down on a piece of paper; I told her to tell me her answer, and then I would show her the piece of paper. After a while of hedging, she told me she was going to kill herself, and that she was losing weight to fit into the coffin. Then I showed her the piece of paper. She cried and cried, knowing that the Lord had shown her a miracle. We prayed for release and that the Lord would heal her. We went over a number of the issues we had prayed about the previous time, and Mary left somewhat relieved.

Mary and I had another miracle some weeks later. Nothing was changing and she was in bad shape. She could not go up and down the basement stairs, she hadn't cooked in ages, she had memory loss, she often couldn't think or plan, and she slept all the time and was depressed. We prayed and asked the Lord to help us through the Holy Spirit (Become God Focused). The Lord reminded me of the car accident (Identify), and I was prompted to ask what portion of her spine was injured. When she told me, I went to get a spinal alignment chart and compared the effects of misalignment. She had every symptom. I knew she had tried everything and that she was reluctant to go to any more doctors, but I had to ask anyway. I asked if she would see a chiropractor for her neck, and she agreed. The next day she went for her first treatment. That day was the first time she cooked a meal in ages; it was the first time she went up and down her basement stairs in ages. She felt great, and boy did I hear about it.

It is wonderful when the Lord does things like that for his people. It was a simple process of asking and listening, and acting on the answers. Forgiveness was key. Release of anger and guilt was essential.

4. Kora Lynne's Story

This is another story about a miracle of the Lord's healing. Kora Lynne's story is probably my favorite, because it was so simple how the Lord answered our prayers. It showed – or should I say, the Lord showed me – that asking is such a simple thing to do, but that we don't do it. It almost seems *too* simple. We want more complicated things. I myself have always wanted a lightning bolt, so that I don't miss what the Lord is saying.

Kora Lynne came in one day, along with her parents. They were at their wits end. She was very depressed, and she had attempted suicide. The psychiatrist had prescribed medicine for her, but it was only amplifying the problem. Kora Lynne had moved to Alberta because things were not working for her in eastern Canada; she had a husband and a little son of three.

During the first interview, I merely collected background information about family, friends, her parents, and her siblings. What stuck out in the conversation was her fear and what we found to be the source of her fear. I had asked what she remembered about her fears, and she told me a story about a nightmare and the incidents surrounding it. Fear was a central issue for Kora Lynne. An example of her fear was her inability to go anywhere alone. If she was in a restaurant and someone laughed across the way, she felt they were laughing at her.

I only saw her four times. The second time we prayed for about 20 minutes (Becoming God Focused). I asked her to bring up the nightmare incident to mind, and as she did we asked for the Lord to clean and fill it (Cleaning and Filling).

As I remember it, she saw herself in her bed and she saw a scary face. She said it was very real and that it was the Devil.

She awoke frightened, and she went to her parents' bedroom with the desire to jump into bed with them. When she got there, however, they just quieted her down and sent her back to bed. She wanted to get in-between them, but never made it, and ended up spending the night on the couch in the living room. Can you imagine a little girl of eight, afraid, alone, and with an active imagination? She became scared of the dark in that room that night.

She ended up with three problems that night (Identification Stage). First, there was the original fear from the dream. Second, there was rejection from her parents. She was a little girl who wanted love from her parents when she was frightened, but they did not give her what she needed. Finally, afraid and rejected, she picked up fear of the dark. We had sourced the major issues, with the help of the Lord; these were central to her present problems.

Next, we prayed through each portion of the evening – her nightmare, the incident in her parent's bedroom, and the time on the couch. As we asked the Lord to touch each negative thing in the experiences, we both began to notice changes. (Cleaning and Filling)

I remember the parent's bedroom scene the best. When Kora Lynne brought it to memory, I could feel the fear rippling off the hair on my arms. Have you ever noticed when someone is afraid or angry around you, you can feel their feelings? Well I definitely could that day.

When people have trouble believing me, I ask them if they can tell when someone in the family is not themself. You don't have to ask them, "how are you?" You just automatically know when they walk in the room. You can tell when someone is happy, or when someone is angry or sad. So when Kora Lynne felt the fear in her memory, I could feel it too. It was powerfully strong. We started praying and asking the Lord to take away the fear and the rejection (Cleaning). We asked him to forgive the parents, and I made sure Kora Lynne wasn't holding on to any resentment. She wasn't. Then we asked the Lord to fill her up with love and to connect her up to her parents and the Lord with little cords of love (Filling). In my imagination the cords would have been like umbilical cords. It was then that I noticed that the fear was gone.

I asked Kora Lynne what was happening and she described the picture she was seeing. Some people see pictures, but it is not necessary. Whatever way the Lord works is just fine; just let Him do the healing work in whatever way He wants. Kora Lynne saw herself kneeling at the foot of the bed and there was a smile on her face. The fear was gone and I knew the Lord had done it. Was I ever excited!

I realized we had found a major source, and that the Lord had showed it to us and healed it. I felt that we should go on and get the fear of the dark, and so we went through the same thing. Kora Lynne brought up the memory of herself on the couch; the fear was back, but not as strong. Then we prayed, asking the Lord to clean and fill it. That was it. Twenty minutes. Kora Lynne left and I knew she had received a powerful healing.

I saw her two more times after that, just to check in and make sure she used the system of The Five Fold Cycle. The third time she saw me she came in on her own, having just been out shopping by herself; she was a changed person. Is that a miracle? Kora Lynne thinks so! (She thanks the Lord).

Although they are miracles, from these stories you can see how easily The Five Fold Cycle works. You open yourself to the Lord in prayer, you ask for the help of the Holy Spirit, and listen for directions and insights. You ask the Lord to clean the negatives away and to fill up the people involved with the positives. The Lord comes through. Often it is a process, but as you keep touching things they lift off and gradually the complete healing occurs. Be patient and persistent.

5. What About Sexual Issues?

I have used the Five Fold Cycle on a number of sexual issues: abuse, homosexuality, exhibitionism, an incest abuser, and more. It seems that the channel for the Lord's healing comes to us by finding the source for the issues[14]. Scripture puts it in a picture for us:

> "See to it that no one fails to obtain the grace of God; that no root of bitterness springs up and causes trouble, and through it many become defiled." (Hebrews 12:15)

Scripture states that the root of bitterness must not take hold; but what is the root of bitterness? It is anger, fear, not getting love the right way, loneliness, guilt, sadness, abuse, trauma, timidness, being put down, and being unaffirmed. I have found that the root can be any single event or a combination of events. When the root of bitterness takes hold, we are not experiencing the love of God and the fruit of the Spirit is not present and active. I like to say that Jesus isn't there in that moment of time, or at least not as much as He could be. When we let Him in, He transforms the bitterness to blessings.

a) The Homosexual

Here is the story of Jim, who started to wonder about his homosexual identity and was disturbed by the many social conflicts it posed. The composite picture of his homosexuality is described like this: Jim found himself attracted to males, particularly to youthful athletic fellows about twenty years younger than him. Jim was a mature citizen and a successful business man. The youth he related to were mature and responsible as well. In fact, no one would have any inclination that either was homosexual; both were satisfied with their situation until the Holy Spirit touched Jim – then the roots of bitterness became apparent. Through prayer, Jim found the root - the loneliness in his early school years. At the same period of childhood he was hospitalized for a hernia and hydrocele (water in the scrotum). The combination lead to bitterness taking root – I call it being 'stuck'. The loneliness caused him to be stuck, fixated at that childhood age, and with an interest in younger males. He had never filled this need. The sickness and operation tied him to self-interest and a phallic fixation.

What were the roots of bitterness in Jim's case? They were childhood loneliness, a need for youthful male company – which could be described as a fixation on immature males – and a phallic interest. You will remember the diagram of the "Water Glass and Cube Theory", where a number of issues – roots, in this case – are stuck together and move as one. Our job in this stage is to identify and separate the problems and issues into small manageable portions, and then take them one by one to the Lord.

Through prayer, the Lord gradually healed Jim's 'little child' with love to replace the loneliness (Cleaning and Filling). It was a process of allowing the Lord's healing into each of Jim's memories and emotions, gradually nibbling away at the multiple issues that lead to the homosexual orientation and identity; the Lord's healing also was applied to the attraction to young men. This took the longest of the healing.

The healing and transformation began with a realization that the lifestyle and behaviors were not fulfilling for Jim, that wholeness and healing meant living a heterosexual life. It took four years of work to heal the intricacies; it meant nibbling away at the many little issues that blocked the Lord's light from the many homosexual thoughts, interests, choices, and behaviors.[15]

b) The Abused Child

I received a distraught call one day from a young mother of a beautiful five year old. She had been unable to get help for her young son, who she found out had been abused by an older boy at day-care.

Jess, age five, was described by his mother as a gentle child who always smiled and was extremely good-natured. Her beautiful child had turned into a monster: always angry, fighting, moody, and pulling kids' pants down in the school yard.

At first they didn't know what had happened – Jess wouldn't talk. They saw the change in behavior, but had no idea what had occurred. One weekend he was at his grandfather's house with his little three year old cousin. The grandfather went upstairs to see what the kids were up to and found the five year old on top of the three year old, trying to perform a sexual act. The grandfather blew-up and screamed; the mother said it wasn't a nice scene. From this incident they were able to find out from Jess what had happened to him: a young male of thirteen had taken Jess downstairs and forcibly molested him. Child Welfare was booked up and there was going to be a four or five week wait for counseling.

The parents came in with their son. Jess sat on his father's lap and his mother was nearby. Seeing how Jess was not very verbal, the parents and I prayed (Become God Focused). We attempted to figure out what had happened in detail (Identify). The parents were very intuitive and could imagine just about every detail – from the force used when taking him down the stairs, to their son being held on a throw rug with his hands outstretched, and feeling the pain of the molestation (Use of the Gifts of the Holy Spirit).

We prayed for each incident as they came to light (Cleaning). We prayed that the Lord would take away fear and apprehension when the boy was coming down the stairs and into the basement. We prayed that the Lord would forgive the thirteen year old boy who had molested him. We asked the Lord why the boy hurt their son, and it was apparent to all of us that he had been hurt as a child and sodomized. We asked the Lord to come into his life and heal him, as well. We prayed for Jess' physical hurt and pain. The parents forgave him. We prayed that the feelings of bondage (being forcibly held down) would leave; and we went through the incident in detail (Cleaning and Filling).

I felt a prompting from the Lord that the little boy should be involved. We asked Jess what he would say to the boy if he were sitting across from him. He lifted his finger and waved it at the empty chair saying, "you shouldn't have hurt me". It was cute, but it was from the child's own hurt. Then I asked him if he forgave the older boy, and with no hesitation he said "yes". We said a prayer of thanks (Thanked the Lord).

That was all we did in prayer. The Lord answered our prayers with fine results. The mother reported that the very next day his behavior had changed, and a week later it was still stable. The mother was concerned about an inordinate interest in sexual matters. Although the problem had been healed by the Lord, the young child had been left with an interest beyond his years. I advised the mother to tell him the facts when he asked questions. All that had happened was that an area of knowledge had opened up before it normally would have. It is not a problem, as long as it is treated with maturity and not squeamishness and fear. The mother understood. A year later he remained okay.

6. Dealing with Feelings, Emotions, or Pressures

The story that comes to me is of a lady of fifty-plus years; I have never been able to track down who she was or where she is living. I tell this story because I have heard a number just like it throughout my work. It will have to be a composite, because permission to share it is not possible. I will call her Trina.

Trina was a beautiful lady. She was mature, spiritual, successful, and busy. Trina had everything from a worldly point of view; she had a house that was paid for, children raised and doing fine, a good job, and she had the Lord's love in her life. So why would she come to a counsellor, I wondered? Trina had everything; she looked and sounded good. But there was a little nagging problem she had never figured out, and it drove her to distraction, and eventually to me. She expressed it this way: "I have everything and I should be happy, but I have this problem. I have a feeling that comes over me, that when I will really need someone, there won't be anyone there!"

Now that is a serious problem and robbed her of peace. She would be going along in her life and the world would be fine, when suddenly this feeling would come over her to rob her of the Lord's Peace. We prayed (Become God Focused).

We asked the Lord for insight and were given it (Identify). It came in two simple numbers: 'five' and 'three' (Gift of Knowledge through the Holy Spirit). I knew from experience that these meant ages. We prayed that the Holy Spirit would give Trina the memories that were attached.

The first memory was easy. She remembered her sister was to be born and her folks had to rush her mother off to the hospital. They told her that she would have to stay home and that they would be back, and not to worry. She was left alone. Now I don't know if you should leave a five year old alone; I wouldn't. But they did.

She remembers walking through the house and up the stairs. There was a wooden banister and she looked through it. She remembers standing at her parents' bedroom door and looking into it, but there was nobody there. That was the first experience that came to memory. We asked the Lord to take that feeling away and give the little girl what she needed at that point, which was love (Cleansing/Filling). It seemed simple and we knew that this was not the initial incident, but it had amplified the original incident. We could not find any other memory so we prayed that the Lord would open up the memories to her. We thanked the Lord and she went home (Thank Him).

Two days later there was a message on my answering machine; she had remembered it. I phoned her back to check in and she told me her story; it was cute and childish. Her sister and she had been playing out in the farm yard near the root cellar. Her sister was mad at her, and as a result locked her in the root cellar. Hmm. Not nice. Of course since the sister was mad, she left her for a while. She must have come back at one point, or Trina would never have made it to my office. It was a relatively simple incident and not an unusual event with farm kids. I have prayed for a few incidents like this one.

Can you imagine the feeling of a little three year old down the root cellar? As she looked around, she would be feeling hurt, scared, lonely, and not enjoying the dampness! The thought that stuck in her mind was, 'when I really need someone there isn't anyone there'. She was caught with that thought, feeling, and conclusion. It is that simple.

We didn't have to pray about it because she had already done her homework and called her sister long distance by phone. They prayed and the Lord healed both of them.

It is quite simple how the Method of Healing Personal Hurt worked for Trina. We simply asked and received. It all started with a problem, one of an emotional or psychological nature. We took that problem to the Lord in prayer, asking for help and having no idea where it would take us. The Holy Spirit guided our thoughts to a few specific ages, and then the Holy Spirit guided Trina's thoughts to specific memories. Then she prayed for healing.

You will note that I wasn't there in the last part. This shows me four things: first, I am not the healer, and the gifts of the Holy Spirit are not mine. The healing comes from God through Jesus Christ, and the gifts are available to anyone who asks.

Second, is that God uses the community to heal. Trina could not get through this one herself; she had tried and was unsuccessful in finding the source alone. She came to me to access the Lord through my gifts. Everyone has gifts and they are for the community. We don't own them and we are responsible to God and the community for their proper use.

> "Now there are varieties of gifts, but the same Spirit; and there are varieties of services, but the same Lord; and there are varieties of activities, but it is the same God who activates all of them in everyone. To each is given the manifestation of the Spirit for the common good."
> (1 Corinthians 12:4-7)

Thirdly, God works directly with the individual. God does not need anyone as a channel if we but open to him. He had used me to help, but in the end Trina's own prayer brought out the final results. She remembered the *Root of Bitterness*. So God can and does deal with us directly, and we do not need specialists, counsellors, healers, pastors or priests.

Fourthly, God leads if we let him. Our job is to be open, to open our will. God will then guide us and direct us, but we must be open to the promptings. God uses His people and the world around us.

A little sister at the Ursuline Retreat Centre in Great Falls, Montana, described the concept of God's relationship to us for me one morning after breakfast. Sister Ursula Marie said, "We are the spoiled children of the good God". As I finish this work, I was struck by her message and wanted to share it with you.

7. My Prayer

My prayer for you is that the Lord will bless you, heal you, and bring you to wholeness as you adhere to His direction:

> "You were taught to put away your former way of life, your old self, corrupt and deluded by its lusts, and to be renewed in the spirit of your minds, and to clothe yourselves with the new self, created according to the likeness of God in true righteousness and holiness." (Ephesians 4:22-24 and Colossians 3:9-10)

God bless you on your journey.
Ken

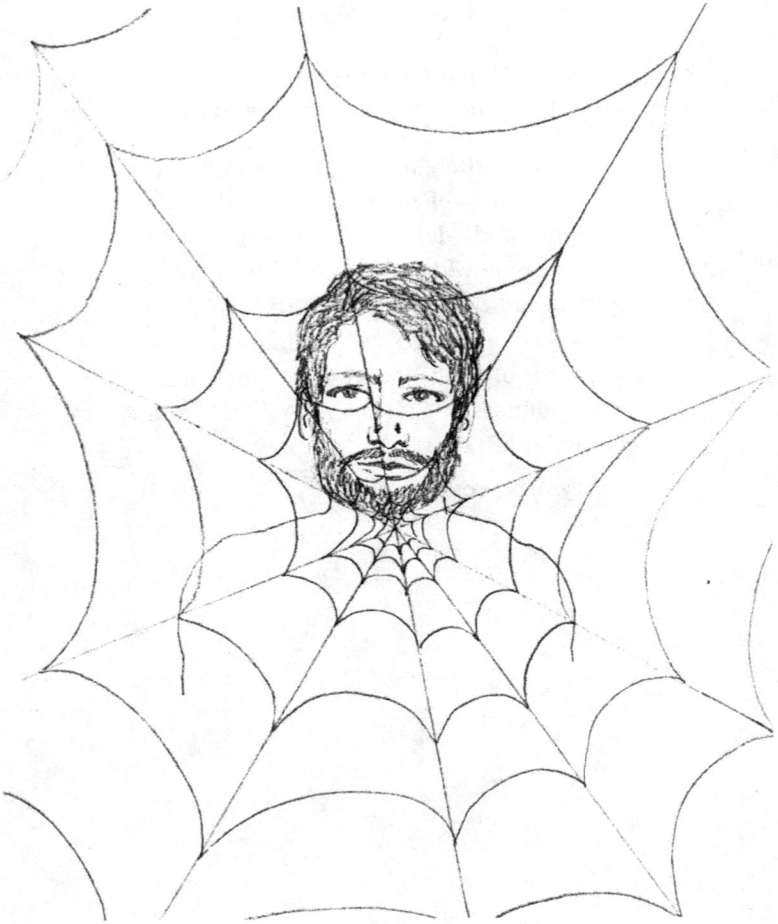

NOTES:

[1] HEALING PERSONAL HURT – DEFINITION / EXPLANATION

'Healing Personal Hurt' has been referred to by many names: "Inner Healing", "Healing of Memories" and "Healing of Emotions", "Soul Healing", "Healing Soul Wounds", etc.

Whatever you might call it, it refers to those hurts, emotional wounds, decisions and actions that result from events in our lives such as failure, rejection, abandonment, abuse, neglect, violence, insecurity and being embarrassed, shamed, terrorized, scared, manipulated, dominated or controlled. All are emotional wounds and all are negative underlying motivations for our actions and behavior.

In 'Healing Personal Hurt', Jesus heals those past hurts; He transforms the memories, He removes the pain and gives us New Life. He replaces the decisions and understandings we formed in the hurt and replaces them with His Truth. Through Jesus' Cross we are healed.

[2] 1 Thess. 5:23 refers to a division of Body, Soul and Spirit. I find it easier to understand the scripture by dividing Soul into two parts - mind and soul. I see Soul being the receptor for blessings and sin. I see

mind as a separate division including thoughts, memories, will, and emotions.

Heb. 4:12 refers to the word of God being keener than a two edged sword cutting between Spirit and Soul.

[3] "By contrast, the fruit of the Spirit is love, joy, peace, patience, kindness, generosity, faithfulness, gentleness, and self-control. There is no law against such things. (Gal. 5:22-23).

[4] Hampsch, Fr. John H., "The Touch Of The Spirit". Fr. Hampsch is a Claretian Missionary Priest based in Los Angeles.

[5] Fr. Robert DeGrandis is a member of the Society of St. Joseph. He is presently involved in a full-time teaching, leadership training and healing ministry around the world. He is a member of the Association of Christian Therapists.

[6] Dennis and Rita Bennett are pioneers in the Episcopal Charismatic Renewal. Please refer to Appendix 'D' for more information.

[7] Soul here is meant the receptor for the residue of sin and the receptor for grace, the result of good action and choice.

[8] Fr. Robert DeGrandis is a member of the Society of St. Joseph. Fr. DeGrandis co-authored some of the books with Betty Tapscott. Please refer to Appendix 'D' for more information.

[9] Scanlan and Cirner and other authors are listed under Deliverance in Appendix 'D'.

[10] Author's note: A recommended therapy is the use of Fr. John H. Hampsch's teaching on "Scripture as Medicine' found in Appendix E.

[11] Author's note: Systems Theory is described as an approach to thinking that has circular causality: linear causality, openness, inter-activeness, and units that react to certain implicit rules and results.

[12] Author's Note: I recommend that you get Fr. DeGrandis' book 'Forgiveness and Inner Healing'. Read one prayer in the morning and the other in the evening for thirty days. As you read the prayer, be attentive to problems/issues that come to your mind. These are promptings of the Holy Spirit. Take each through the Five Fold Cycle. It works - try it!

[13] 'Transforming Problems' is a book by Bert Ghezzi in the Supplemental Readings - Appendix 'D'.

[14] This book is not meant to be a forum for discussion of homosexuality, but rather to explain how healing has occurred in individuals who have chosen to overcome unwanted same-sexual attractions.

I, Kenneth, have found that healing has occurred in individuals who have chosen to overcoming unwanted same-sexual attractions.

I take the position that biological, psychological and social factors shape sexual identity at an early age for most people. Further that there is no such thing as a "gay gene" and there is no evidence to support the idea that homosexuality is simply genetic. This position then opens the field to healing and wholeness through Jesus Christ.

[15] I refer you to http://www.narth.com the website for the National Association for Research and Therapy of Homosexuality, NARTH. This site is now being redirected to www.therapeuticchoice.com. On that site you can find many scientific and professional studies examining homosexuality:

- *NARTH's Response to the American Psychological Association's Claims on Homosexuality.* – This paper examines over 100 years of scientific literature on the subject of overcoming unwanted sexual attractions.

- *Identical Twin Studies Demonstrate Homosexuality is Not Genetic* by Dr. Neil Whitehead.

- *Practice Guidelines for the Treatment of Unwanted Same-Sex Attractions and Behavior*
- These guidelines are intended for the treatment of clients who experience unwanted same-sex attractions (SSA) and behavior.

- *Right to Treatment* – The NARTH Alliance respects each client's dignity, autonomy and free agency. We believe that clients have the right to claim a gay identity, or to diminish their homosexuality and to develop their heterosexual potential.

[16] This is a teaching, used with permission, from the vast resource of Fr. John Hampsch, CMF, Claretian Teaching Ministry, http://catholicbooks.net/

Appendix 'A'
The Five Fold Cycle: Method Of Healing Personal Hurt

(A PROBLEM SOLVING METHOD)

I have started training people to do housecleaning. It goes like this:

When we are hurt, there are 3 negative reactions:

1. Unforgiveness - Anger, bitterness, resentment and the like is the first major problem.

2. Guilt - which is self-pity, uncertainty, not forgiving self, worry, anxiety, tension caused by worry is the second problem.

3. Depression - This is a symptom of the previous two and therefore when you deal with #1 and #2, depression leaves on its own.

Process:

The answer to how to deal with these is easy if you believe in Christ's help. It goes through a Five Fold Cycle.

1. Become God Focused: Focus on God in prayer praise and thanksgiving. Ask for the gifts of the Spirit, which include wisdom, knowledge and understanding. Be humble and penitent.

2. Identify: Identify problems and be specific. Ask for wisdom and knowledge from the Lord. Look for specific sources for the problems and expand on them. Often problems interconnect, so make sure to separate and individualize them. Do things one at a time. It is a process of healing.

3. Clean: Do something.

| C |
| L |
| E |
| A |
| N |
| S |
| E |

- Forgive where forgiveness is needed.
- Forgive others, God and self
- Bind any spiritual involvement.
- Confess and ask for cleansing.
- Give up the problem to the Lord, e.g.: anxiety / worry / etc.
- Ask the Lord to take it away.
- It is often important to actually follow through by personal contact with the parties involved. Be sensitive to the Lord's direction in this matter.
- It is good to take these matters to the Communion Table and repeat the process.

What we are doing in this section is gradually nibbling away at the problem areas. Remember you cannot deal with depression because it is a symptom and often very global in nature.

4. Fill:

> **B**
> **L**
> **E**
> **S**
> **S**
> **I**
> **N**
> **G**

- Ask for the in-filling of the Holy Spirit.
- Ask for the contrasting good characteristics.
- Ask for the blessings and gifts to fill the space left when you cleansed yourself in # 3.
- Prayer and Scripture reading are important.
- Make sure to ask for blessings for others you have cleansed. They also need the gifts and blessings.
- Ask the Lord to heal the hurt.
- Take it to Communion or Eucharist.

If you clean the areas/problems and do nothing to replace them with positives, there is a high probability that you can slip back into the same old routines. You must fill the place that has been cleaned up, with the good things from God through his Holy Spirit.

5. Go back to # 1. Stop focusing on yourself. Thank the Lord.

Appendix 'B'
The Holy Spirit And The Gifts Of The Holy Spirit

To understand Inner Healing and to use it effectively, you need to use and be active in the Gifts of the Holy Spirit. Some will call it "Born of the Spirit", others "Baptized in the Spirit", but all understand that we have received an out pouring of the Holy Spirit and the Gifts have become operative in our life.

There are three relationships in God: There is a relationship with the Father, creator and first person of the Trinity. The question that I often pose is this: "Do you have a Relationship with the Father?" And the next question I ask is: "By what name does He call you?" The Father calls me Ken or Kenny, and sometimes son – special son. It is a familiar kind of call to me.

The next one looks at Jesus, the incarnate Son of God, the second person of the blessed Trinity. The question I pose about connection to Jesus is: "Do you have a Personal Relationship with Jesus Christ?" And further I ask "by what name does He call you?" Jesus calls me friend. In my imagination we are quite close. Once in a Healing prayer about loneliness, I saw him on the back of the bicycle I was driving. His hair just flowed out to the back as we sped along the street in Medicine Hat,

Alberta. I was 10 or 12 years old. Beautiful image, and in that memory there is no more loneliness!

The third person of the Trinity is the Holy Spirit. He is to dwell inside us. Our body is the temple of the Holy Spirit.

> "Or do you not know that your body is a temple of the Holy Spirit within you, which you have from God, and that you are not your own? For you were bought with a price; therefore glorify God in your body."
> (1 Corinthians 6:19-20)

The indwelling Holy Spirit lives in us and His gifts become operative in our life. When I received the Holy Spirit at a Life In the Spirit Seminar, I found God became interactive in my life. I would pray and I would see His actions in my life. They came in words, in visions, by changes in my thoughts and actions, and God-incidents in my life – God became interactive.

The following page has a brief explanation of the Holy Spirit and His gifts.

UNDERSTANDING THE GIFTS

1. <u>What is meant by Charismatic Gifts?</u>
   A charismatic gift is a manifestation of God's power and presence given freely, for God's honor and glory and for the service of others.
   Specifically the term refers to manifestations of the power of the Holy Spirit mentioned in the Scriptures, especially after Pentecost, and which have always remained with the Church in both her teaching and practice.

2. How many Charismatic Gifts are there?

Since the Charismatic Gifts are manifestations of the Holy Spirit, it is impossible to say how many there are. Scripture provides a number of lists of offices and ministries. The classical list, used by most, is St. Paul's in 1 Corinthians 12:8-10, where nine gifts are described. These nine seem to be normal ministries that should be present in every local church.

3. List and describe these nine gifts.

The nine gifts, according to the usual threefold division are:

A. THE WORD GIFTS (The Power to Say)

a) The Gift of Tongues -- whereby the person gives God's message, in a language unknown to him, for the community present. This Gift also includes a prayer language used for person prayer. It is a multiple gift of languages with multiple purposes.

b) The Gift of Interpretation -- whereby a person, after the use of the gift of tongues, gives the general meaning of what the person has said, or a response to what has been said. Interpretation can also be used privately in conjunction with the gift of prayer tongues.

c) The Gift of Prophecy -- whereby the person gives God's message in the vernacular for the community or for an individual.

B. THE SIGN GIFTS (The Power To Do)

a) The Gift of Faith -- which enables the person at a given moment to believe, and to call upon God's power with a certainty that excludes all doubt.

b) The Gift of Healing -- which enables the person to be God's instrument in bringing

about the well-being of another, on one or more
levels, spiritual, psychological or physical.

c) The Gift of Miracles-- which enables a person to
be God's instrument in either an instant healing or in
some other powerful manifestation of God's power.

C. THE INTELLECTUAL GIFTS (The Power to Know)

The Word of Wisdom-- whereby a person is granted
an insight into God's plan in a given situation and is
enabled to put into words of advice or of direction.

The Word of Knowledge-- whereby a person is
granted an insight into a divine mystery or facet of
man's relation to God and is enabled to put this into
a word that helps others to grasp the mystery.

The Gift of Discernment-- whereby a person is enabled
to know the source of an inspiration or action, whether
it came from the Holy Spirit or from the evil spirit.

Appendix 'C'
Every Negative Becomes
A Positive In The Cross

FIVE FOLD CYCLE: METHOD OF HEALING PERSONAL HURT

Every time there is a negative we take it to the Lord – asking Him in!

1. Ask the Lord into the problem - We focus on God in prayer praise and thanksgiving.

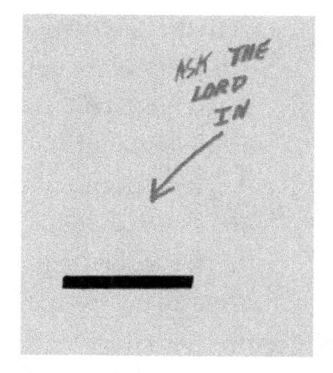

Ask for the gifts of the Spirit, which include wisdom, knowledge and understanding. Be penitent.

2. Identify problems and be specific.

Ask for wisdom and knowledge from the Lord. Look for specific sources for the problems and expand on them. (Basic problem solving method.)
Often problems interconnect. Do things one at a time.

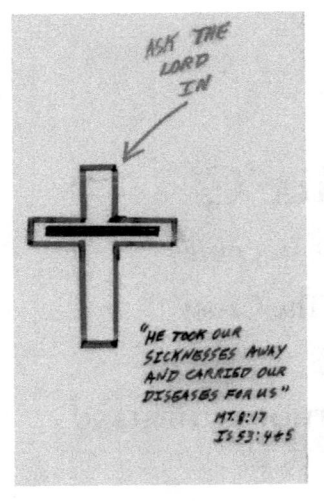

3. Clean:
- Forgive where forgiveness is needed
- Forgive others, God and self
- Bind any spiritual involvement.
- Confess and ask for cleansing.
- Give up the problem to the Lord, e.g.: anxiety / worry
- Ask the Lord to take it away.

4. Fill the empty spot with God's Blessings:
- Ask for the in-filling of the Holy Spirit.
- Ask for the contrasting good characteristics.
- Ask for the blessings and gifts to fill the space left when you cleansed yourself in # 3.
- Prayer and Scripture reading are important.
- Make sure to ask for blessings for others you have cleansed. They also need the gifts and blessings.
- Ask the Lord to Heal the hurt.
- Take it to Communion or Eucharist.

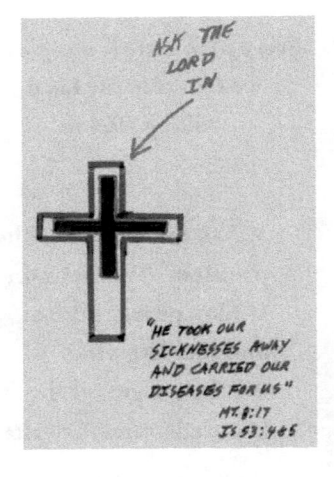

5. Go back to # 1. Stop focusing on yourself. Thank the Lord.

Appendix 'D'
Supplemental Readings

1. Inner Healing References:

Bertolucci, John. *Healing: God's Work Among Us*. Ann Arbor: Servant Books, 1987.

DeGrandis, Robert, *Brokeness To Life*. DeGrandis, Robert. *Forgiveness And Inner Healing*.

DeGrandis, Robert. *Forgiveness Is Divine*.

Ghezzi, Bert. *Transforming Problems*. Ann Arbor: Servant Books, 1986.

Green, Thomas H. *Weeds Among The Wheat*. Notre Dame: Ave Maria Press, 1984.

Hampsch, John H. *Healing Of Memories*. (Long Version), (CD) Claretian Teaching Ministry.

Linn, Matthew, and Dennis Linn, and Sheila Fabrican. *Healing The Eight Stage Of Life*. Mahwah: Paulist Press, 1965.

Macnutt, Francis. *Healing*. Notre Dame: Ave Maria Press, 1974.

Pearson, Mark A. *Christian Healing: A Practical Comprehensive Guide.* New Jersey: Chosen Books, 1990.

Sanford, Agnes. *The Healing Light.* Plainfield: Logos International, 1947.

Sandford, John Loren. *The Transformation of the Inner Man.* Tulsa: Victory House, 1982.

Seamands, David. *Healing For Damaged Emotions.* Wheaton: Victor Books, SP Publications, Inc., 1981.

Scanlan, Michael. *Healing Principles.* Ann Arbor: Servant Books, 1987.

Shlemon, Barbara. *Healing The Hidden Self.* Notre Dame: Ave Maria Press, 1982.

Wimber, John and Kevin Spranger. *Power Healing.* New York: Row Publishers, 1987.

2. Gifts of the Holy Spirit References:

Bennett, Dennis. *Nine O'clock In The Morning.* Plainfield: Logos International, 1970.

Bennett, Dennis, et al. *The Holy Spirit And You.* Plainfield: Logos International, 1971.

DeGrandis, Robert. *Coming To New Life.*

DeGrandis, Robert. *An Introduction To The Catholic Charismatic Renewal.*

Hampsch, John H. *The Touch Of The Spirit*. (CD) Claretian Teaching Ministry.

Roycroft, T.W. and Kenneth L. Fabbi. *You Can Minister Spiritual Gifts*. Lethbridge, Alberta, Canada: Kenneth L. Fabbi, 2019.

3. Deliverance References:

Harper, Michael. *Spiritual Warfare*. Watchung: Charisma Books, 1970.

Prince, Derek. *From Curse To Blessing: You Can Choose*. Chosen, 2006.

Prince, Derek. *Spiritual Warfare*. Whitaker House 1987.

Scanlan, Michael and Randall Cirner. *Deliverance From Evil Spirits*. Ann Arbor: Servant Books, 1980.

4. Research Review of Interaction of Religion and Health:

Koenig, McCullough, Larson. *Handbook of Religion and Health*. New York: Oxford Press, 2001.

Appendix 'E'
Scripture as Medicine[16]
The Rx from the Doctor Jesus

We often hear of people giving other people scriptures to help them through the problems they are currently facing. Maybe someone has given you a scripture. But what is the purpose of it? Why do they give each other scriptures? There must be some purpose to this act and some expectation of the one who is giving it. What is expected and what are the potential results?

So let's look at this practice in the Christian circles of giving scriptures; we will begin by looking at one of the four scriptures that give credence to this practice. In this explanation we will see how Jesus expects us to use scripture, the purpose to be accomplished, and how each one of us might use this practice.

First let's look at the scripture that gives meaning to this practice and then we will look at the Rx (prescription) from the doctor, Jesus.

Scripture: Proverbs 4: 20 – 22

> [20] My child, be attentive to my words; incline your ear to my sayings.

> 21 Do not let them escape from your sight; keep them within your heart.
> 22 For they are life to those who find them, and healing to all their flesh.

The doctor – Jesus – gives us the prescription: a plan of action and authoritative direction for our care. Like the Rx from the Doctor.

The first lines of the scripture are directed to us personally. It says 'My son', or 'My daughter'. It is calling us in accordance to our adoptive relationship to Jesus. We are adoptive sons and daughters, heirs to the kingdom.

Jesus' first directive in verse 20 is 'be attentive'. Today one might say 'pay attention, I have something to say!' In scripture the Lord is saying *pay attention.*

Pay attention to what? The Lord is saying, 'pay attention to My words'. Jesus, the doctor, is telling us to pay attention to His words. What words and where are they? They are in the scriptures. Jesus is telling us to pay attention to His words in the scriptures.

In the next portion of verse 20, Jesus says 'incline your ear to them'. Can you see all the people with their heads bent, inclining their ears? No! It means 'hearing them': hear the scriptures.

Already you might be noting that Jesus, the doctor Jesus, is giving particular instruction. It is the Rx from the doctor. And He is discussing our different modalities.

> First: Attention – be attentive to my words.
> Second: Hearing – incline your ear.
> Third: Sight – do not let them escape from your sight.
> Fourth: Heart – keep them within your heart.

Jesus is going over four modalities, to which we must apply the scriptures. He is telling us to pay attention – keep them in our attention; always keeping them in our focus and running through our mind.

Next He is saying 'hear them'. Well to hear them, we have to say them. We know that when you are studying and you read something, if you say it and hear it, the odds are they will stay in our mind longer; Memory is increased.

Next, Jesus says 'keep them in your sight'. Put scriptures in places that you will see them. If you're a driver, put them on your dash. If you are a computer nerd, put them on the monitor. Put them on the fridge, the mirror, your T-shirt, etc. When we see them, they remind us of the message. The more often we see them, the more we remember them.

You will remember the old computer line: "Garbage In – Garbage Out". It is the same principle with attention, sight, and hearing. The more good things we put in to our minds, vision, and hearing, the more that will be stored inside and the more likely that they will be there when we need them.

Finally, Jesus says 'keep them in your heart'. What does that mean? It means to ponder on them, to stir them around inside. The heart is the storehouse of what we put into it and from it comes what is stored. Remember that the Scripture says the Virgin Mary stored these things in her heart.

Take a look at Matthew and Luke:

Matthew 12:34 - You brood of vipers! How can you speak good things, when you are evil? For out of the abundance of the heart the mouth speaks.

Luke 6:45 - The good person out of the good treasure of the heart produces good, and the evil person out of evil treasure produces evil; for it is out of the abundance of the heart that the mouth speaks.

<u>Let us summarize to this point:</u>

The doctor, Jesus, is instructing us, His followers, to do four things with Scripture:

Keep them in our *Attention – Hearing – Sight –* and *Heart*

Why? Why does He want us to keep them in our Attention, hearing, sight, and heart? There is an expectation to every prescription! I refer you to verse 22 of Proverbs 4:

22 For they are life to those who find them, and healing to all their flesh.

This is the promise from Doctor Jesus. It is a twofold promise; promising life and health.

If we keep His Words in our *Attention – Hearing – Sight – and Heart,* they will give us life. Life's energy, vitality, hope, the strength to go on, etc. As well, if we keep His Words in our *Attention – Hearing – Sight – and Heart,* they will give health to our whole body.

You can understand this by looking at common issues in people's lives. If you worry you may get ulcers; if you are angry, you are more likely to get heart attacks. So by simple logic we can know, if you hold good things in your *Attention – Hearing – Sight – and Heart,* they will cause good effects on your body. Your body defenses will be built up and be able to fight back. It's really quite simple.

The Rx from the Doctor Jesus:

Keep my Word in your *Attention – Hearing – Sight – and Heart*

The Promise:
It will give *you* life and health.

How do you apply the direction from the doctor?

It is simple, as is all things of Jesus. You take the area in your life where you are struggling, and find the scripture that speaks to it. You keep this scripture in your attention, hearing, sight, and heart. This is an example of the 'Filling' in the Five Fold Cycle. As you do, the problem will dissipate, life will come back to this area, and healing will occur.

My brother, Ron, uses this method and teaches others to use it as well. When an issue comes up, say fear, he gathers scripture relating to fear and writes them on flip cards, as you would when you are studying at school or university. He carries them in his shirt pocket. Whenever there is a free spot in the day, or an intermission in the TV program, he pulls the cards out and reads them, thinks about them, ponders them, and listens to them as he speaks them out loud. It works!

The process is simply applying scripture to the problem and letting scripture, (God's love), push the garbage out of our minds, our attention, our hearing, our sight, and our hearts.

What happens when we follow the doctor's direction? We receive the fruit of our compliance. The promise: *"They are life to those who find them"* and *"health to a man's whole body."* They give healing and health throughout the body.

Here is another story to embellish this method of Scripture as Medicine.

And then there was John

John had these sexual ideas floating around in his head all the time. Every time there was a pause in his thinking or attention, sexual thoughts would pop into his mind. He could not stop it. John tried playing music all the time or fighting the thoughts, but sooner or later with their constant badgering, he would start giving way and would find himself in a full blown fantasy about sexual pleasures. Embarrassed and ashamed, John would come before God and beg for forgiveness, promising never to follow the thoughts again, but it just repeated and repeated as the thoughts and images took over his mind.

John knew that all his efforts and focus could not stop this spiritual assault; he said he had tried everything. So together we walked through the Five Fold Cycle, looking for the source and cleansing. When we came to the time for filling, it became obvious that he needed a tool to use over and over as each thought or image came into his head. Scripture, using the sword of the spirit, is a great weapon to fight and defend.

> Indeed, the word of God is *living and active*, sharper than any two-edged sword, piercing until it divides soul from spirit, joints from marrow; *it is able to judge the thoughts and intentions of the heart.* - Hebrews 4: 12 *(Italics are put in by the author)*

So John prayed and asked for a scripture he might use each time his mind was attacked. The scripture came quickly:

> Thy word is a lamp unto my feet, and a light unto my path. - Psalm 119:105 (KJV)

The direction for healing was that each time a thought or image came to mind, John was to say this simple psalm. John found that each time he said the psalm the ideas would disappear and gradually the thoughts and images lessened. It was a battle he won using scripture as medicine from Doctor Jesus.

Try this prescription Rx from Doctor Jesus and use 'Scripture as Medicine' in your own life!